Evensong

Evensong

Ingrid Wendt

New Odyssey Series
Truman State University Press
Kirksville, MO

Copyright © 2011 Truman State University Press, Kirksville, Missouri, 63501
All rights reserved
tsup.truman.edu

Cover art: Gray Jacobik, *Evening Light on Snow*, © 2011.

Cover design: Teresa Wheeler

Library of Congress Cataloging-in-Publication Data

Wendt, Ingrid, 1944–
Evensong / Ingrid Wendt.
        p. cm.
ISBN 978-1-935503-93-4 (pbk. : alk. paper) — ISBN 978-1-61248-069-5 (ebook)
I. Title.
PS3573.E516E94 2011
811'.54—dc22

                                                                    2011026622

The paper in this publication meets or exceeds the minimum requirements of the American National Standard for Information Sciences—Permanence of Paper for Printed Library Materials, ANSI Z39.48–1992.

To cherished friends Dorothy and the late William Stafford,
for showing me the ways

To my grandchildren Gemma and Gavino Goette, bright lights

To Ralph, my dearest love for more than forty years

This book is for you

All nature speaks and sings and is musical...
and all animal sounds are a prayer. So is the human voice.
That is why contemplative monks are silent.
They have dedicated their voices to sing only in choir,
because they have understood that the voice is a prayer.
—Ernesto Cardenál

Contents

Acknowledgments

Grateful acknowledgment is made to the editors and publishers of the following magazines and anthologies in which some of these poems first appeared, a few in slightly different form and/or with different titles.

Anthropology and Humanism: "Reserve"

Ascent: "A Gathering"

basalt: "Valse Triste"

Calapooya Collage: "Ashes on the Tongue," "Maybe More Than We Know," "Lesson Plans, Vernal, Utah," "With Ninety-Eight Friends"

Calapooya: "Some Words to Toss Your Direction," "Tree of Joy at the Super"

Chili Verde Review: "Losing in the Mail My Years-Old Copy of Your Specially Autographed Book"

CutBank: "On the Nature of Bach's B Minor Mass"

Drunken Boat: "To a German Painter Who Asked about Poetry's Open Forms"

Ellipsis: "Beyond Argument," "Likeness"

Fireweed: "Mother's Day, Ellensburg, Washington,"

Hubbub: "The Fisherman's Wife"

KSOR Guide to the Arts: "Fan Letter from the Fourth Grade"

Many Mountains Moving: "Jade Plant"

Massachusetts Review: "Poem at Forty-Five"

Mississippi Mud: "The Way It Was"

Ms.: "On the Nature of Touch"

National Poetry Review: "Repartee"

Nimrod: "And the Greatest of These"

Oregon Quarterly: "Tiramisù"

Runes: "Sanctuary"

Poet & Critic: "All We Can Use"

Prairie Schooner: "Benediction"

Painted Hills Quarterly: "This Is His Story"

The Pacific: "Doors"

Tehachapi Review: "Coleus"

Valparaiso Poetry Review: "The Keeper of Secrets," "Armistice"

Victory Park: "Split Couplets for John"

Weber Studies: "Fertility Plant," "Give Us This Day," "Silence"

"Love in Venice" first appeared as "Four Poems of Love" in *Love Poems for the Media Age*, an anthology edited by David Samis (Vancouver, BC: Ripple Effect Press).

"After a Class in Seaweed" first appeared in *No More Masks! An Anthology of Twentieth–Century American Women Poets*, 2nd ed., edited by Florence Howe (New York: HarperCollins).

"Naked" appeared as "Personal Poem" in the first edition of *No More Masks! An Anthology of Twentieth–Century American Women Poets*, edited by Ellen Bass and Florence Howe (New York: Doubleday).

"Sanctuary" was a finalist in the 2006 *Runes* Award competition, and appeared in *Runes* 2007.

"Benediction" was first runner-up in the 2003 Rita Dove Poetry Award, under the title "The Blessing," Joy Harjo, judge.

A shorter, earlier version of "A Gathering" received second place in the national competition "In the Beginning Was the Word" (Portland, OR), September 2002, under the title "For Mary."

The author wishes to thank Hedgebrook Farms, Ft. Langley Washington; the University of New Mexico and the D. H. Lawrence Ranch, Taos, NM; the Rockefeller Study and Conference Center, Bellagio, Italy; the Kulturreferat, Munich, Germany; and the Mary Anderson Center for the Arts, Indiana, for periods of writing time during which some of these poems were begun.

To Gray Jacobik, marvelous poet and painter, and generous friend, my heartfelt thanks for the use of *Evening Light on Snow* on the cover of this book.

Father Ernesto Cardenal of Nicaragua has graciously approved this paraphrase of his eloquent prose, from *To Live is to Love* (New York: Herder & Herder, 1972). I am deeply grateful.

Many thanks to Ursula Le Guin for her generous permission to reprint lines from her poem "Song for Elisabeth," first published in *From Here We Speak: An Anthology of Oregon Poetry*, edited by Ingrid Wendt and Primus St. John (Corvallis: Oregon State University Press, 1993), and reprinted in her *Going Out with Peacocks* (New York: HarperCollins, 1994).

Grateful thanks to Milkweed Editions and Kim Stafford for permission to use lines from *Every War Has Two Losers: William Stafford on Peace and War*, edited and with an introduction by Kim Stafford (Minneapolis: Milkweed Editions, 2003).

The William Stafford lines from "A Ritual to Read to Each Other," are found in *The Way It Is: New and Selected Poems*. © 1960, 1998 by William Stafford and the Estate of William Stafford. Reprinted with the permission of Graywolf Press, Minneapolis, Minnesota, www.graywolfpress.org. My thanks to the publisher and to the Estate of William Stafford.

The line from Theodore Roethke's poem "What Can I Tell My Bones?" is reprinted with the permission of Random House, Inc. The poem appears in *Roethke: Collected Poems* (New York: Doubleday, 1961).

Filmmaker Haydn Reiss, director of *Every War Has Two Losers*—a documentary based on the journals of William Stafford—provided inspiration and helpful details in the writing of "Numbers." Thank you, Haydn—for this, and for your powerful film.

I am greatly indebted to my first piano and organ teacher, the late Frances Sherwood of the Aurora Conservatory of Music, and to the late Dr. Rudolph Ganz, president of Chicago Music College, for patient and invaluable guidance.

To the directors of the choirs, in Eugene, Oregon, and in Frankfurt/Main, with whom I have sung during the past thirty years, as well as to The Motet Singers of Eugene, my humble thanks for your musicianship and fellowship.

Quietly, my teachers at C. M. Bardwell School in Aurora, Illinois—Miss Mitchell, Miss Bloss, Mrs. Kuk, Miss Erickson, Miss Thomas, Miss Michaelson, Miss Langhammer, and Mrs. Reedy—let me know they had faith in me. I hope I've lived up to most of it. In Rose Marie Rockenbach's Oswego High School English class, I discovered that poems could speak to me and for me. I am grateful. The Reverend Drexel Mollison of the New England Congregational Church in Aurora gave me free use of the console organ for practice, as well as trust in my playing for worship services. Reeve Thompson, Oswego High School choral director, provided opportunities to develop my skill as an accompanist. Those experiences are in me forever.

For inspiration, exceptional instruction, and friendship from poet-mentors Robert Dana, William Stafford, and my beloved husband, Ralph Salisbury, enormous gratitude.

Grateful thanks for encouragement and friendship to many poets, scholars, friends, and editors: Frances Payne Adler, Ken Brewer, Edward Byrne, Barbara Crooker, John Daniel, Margarita Donnelly , Barbara Drake, Patricia Fargnoli, Tom Ferté, Annie Finch, Helen Frost, Martha Gatchell, Jerry Gatchell, Palmer Hall, Florence Howe, Dell and Virginia Hymes, Gray Jacobik, Marilyn Krysl, Maxine Kumin, Diane Lockward, Janet McCann, Rodger Moody, Erik Muller, Naomi Shihab Nye, Alicia Ostriker, Myrna Peña-Reyes, Paulann Petersen, Hilda Raz, Kim Stafford, Bill Sweet, Mark Thalman, Patty Wixon, and Vince Wixon; and to Nancy Rediger, outstanding director, and the fine staff of Truman State University Press.

To Kate Sikelianos, the most loyal sister and friend anyone could hope to have, my everlasting appreciation for a lifetime of love and support.

To my beautiful, high-spirited, multilingual daughter, Martina Erin Marie Salisbury, brilliant designer, wise woman, gentle mother: these belated apologies for too often, during your childhood, being more available to the world of words than I was to you. I will be forever grateful for the wonder and joy you have brought to my life, and for all I have learned and keep on learning from you.

To my mother and father, Matilda Helen Kathryn Petzke Wendt and Edward Julius Wendt: you told me I would thank you some day for music lessons and for making me practice. I do thank you. For this and for so much more. Over and over and over.

I.

So are we knit together
By force of opposites,
The daughter that unravels
The skein the mother knots.

One must be divided
So that one be whole,
And this is the duplicity
Alleged of woman's soul.

Ursula K. Le Guin
from "Song for Elisabeth"

Poem at Forty-Five

Summer. July. Hot. And the daredevil spiders,
like an eruption of mushrooms, nightly string the whole of their
faith between the same doomed places:

Volkswagen to Datsun;
picnic table to movable bench; bushes
each side of the front porch step. Look!

These spiders are everywhere. Shiny gold peas,
they'd spin the whole house up if they could.

We'd sleep the ritual hundred years,
we'd have to hack our way out. And yet

each morning I find them
beautiful, go
out of my way to lift, lightly, at least

one nearly invisible polar thread to another,
safer, anchor: each
shimmering, flat, before-Columbus plate of the world

adrift: wheels
within wheels
and the motionless sun at the center,

a solstice
poised in its own
readiness: silent

as some days my own words dissolve
in my hands, middle-aged and amazed
at where they have come from,

where they are going. My daughter,
eighteen, on her own, but connected;

my mother, seventy-eight, on her own,
still, connected; and I

in the knowledge there is no morning
I cannot wake up and find the world
forever changed.

On the Nature of Touch

My daughter's cat in the morning, before he'll eat,
needs to be picked up and petted, cradled (as I used to
carry my daughter) on one hip from pantry to counter
and back to the dish of food that was fresh the first
time he sniffed it, but not good enough.

This cat can be roaming all night, returning ravenous.
This cat can be let outside at first light and stand, moon-
patient, at the door, in rain, until we rise again. His fur
can be six soggy layers of needles and moss on the floor of the Oregon
Coast Range and still the Salmon Supreme we spoon into his dish
holds that scrupulous tongue only an instant before his voice
stalks our slippers, our wonder again at such
hunger for touch that goes beyond all bodily need.

So we stroke him between the ears, stirring up the same food.
And we rub his nose just over the spot where the whiskers sprout,
run our hands repeatedly down the long rapids of his spine
until dander and fur rise like spume, drift in the imperceptible
breath of the furnace, saying Good cat, Good Pillow, Eat.

And my daughter, who hardly could wait to be out on her own,
phones from her student apartment once, maybe twice a day, to ask for my
stroganoff recipe, or if vinegar will, in the absence of cleanser,
clean a greasy sink. She reads me the funnies.
Will I give her a ride to the store? Each day, this

delicate sniffing the ground called *home*; the words we speak
a ritual independent of meaning: thin fingers sifting the rich
humus of memory: bright
splashes of hair dye she left behind
on the downstairs hall carpet, each color a different
year of her life: stones scattered by Gretel to find the way back.

There is no returning to where she has been. How can I
not cradle her; each time she calls, one more blessed

delay on the long, slow road from touching each of us took
for granted those years I held her in my arms at least once a day
and she held me in a gaze that knew nothing but trust: water
disappearing through cracks in my fingers I myself tried, as a child,
over and over to cup and drink clear in my small, close hands.

The Keeper of Secrets

By fair means or foul, they track you down:
those escaped from the lips of strangers

those handed to you on a leash, as though
your ears were cages, secure.

Here's the dirt on a good friend's mother.
How can this good friend still

not know? And Gossip, now yours to release
or lock up forever, tugs, tugs: Tell!

Here's the pride of another
mother: You'll never know what I

put up with, all those years. And three years
after her death, without being called, Sudden

Insight, snarling, sidles
into the pack.

What to do when a foreigner tells you what
she told another: if he's abusive, and law

won't let you divorce, this method:
so easy and safe, it leaves no trace?

Bad dogs, bad dogs, I never
asked to own you and now

must keep you from harm
the rest of my life.

The Fisherman's Wife

You know my story: the flounder my husband
caught, buying his freedom with magic.
Neat trick! True, I'd always wanted
a newer cottage, who among us doesn't
like an easier life? And I was ecstatic,
really, until my husband sauntered

in, smug, and demanded a kiss. More,
if the worst be told. As though
like the flounder, my freedom could be
had at a price; that I should adore
material things so much I'd show
my thanks between my grateful knees.

No matter if the heart was in it.
So why not ask for a bigger house?
A mansion? Palace? Kingdom? I
got everything, knowing of course this
is not what we live for. And of course
I knew I couldn't be God. But try

as I would, until that point no one
would challenge me, no one saw
anything wrong in asking for more than
I needed, in fact they urged me on.
What's protest without an audience?
Why not end it, be truly alone?

Last week walking the beach I found
a glass fishing float. Seven
years it took to travel from Japan.
Fierce, the storm that ripped it out

of the parallel current, sent it
to lie robin's-egg fragile on sand.

Seven years back I never
had heard of a flounder. Three
fishermen lost last week in the storm
were at home in all kinds of weather.
Three wives never could have dreamed of me,
jealous, with no clear right to mourn.

Valse Triste

He, bless him, is trying his everyday best to live,
Stepping right over prognoses. His wife. Her will.
She, God bless her, wants him alive

And he won't wear his jacket. Connives
To watch the sunset without it. Won't take his pills.
Bless him, this man is trying his best each day to live,

To its own conclusion, every *encore* his heart delivers.
You know where he'd be if words could kill,
But do we blame her? She says she wants him alive.

There's nothing she wouldn't deprive
Him of if it helped. His truant feet. His will.
And he, she knows it, does not try his best. He lives

To spite her, to leave her with nothing to give.
She can lay down her life and he'll
Bless God, not she-who-wants-him-alive.

If this goes on she'll never survive.
Nor he. Whose fault? Whose will
Be done? He, trying with every blessed step to die
Without her. She, wanting to want him alive.

Maybe More Than We Know

I, too, can hold my own in the kitchen, indulge
friends and sometimes family with soufflé or quiche, my hands
whole days preparing an evening that goes beyond

simple nutrition. Yes, elegance hooks me. And,
maybe like you, some days I rise to the challenge of
getting through not only dinner but whatever, with something

better than just getting through—whole days
content with surfaces, no
impulse to follow any idea to its source or

conclusion, ignoring those simple, everyday
clicks of recognition flashing
in and out of some place deep in my mind.

Sometimes I feel them complete, though wordless:
almost invisible presences, ribs
like bones of sardines shining through:

brass outlines under the black rubbing paper
of tourists, defining maybe
more than we know, what we are too busy living

to say. Right then
I must go to my desk or lose them forever.
And most of the time they are lost.

Small quasars.
Morning stars
swallowed by sun.

Am I alone in this? Doesn't it happen
sometimes to you? Not poems,
exactly, but moments when something comes clear,

then vanishes. Small
ripples of knowing.
How easy it is to ignore them.

All the little fish of our dreams
nibbling our days
and look how the days go on.

Tiramisù

"*Tiramisù*: Pick Me Up," you translated for us,
but "Heaven on Earth" is what I remembered,
and so it was:

       layers of chocolate sponge cake drenched with rum
and espresso; layers of *mascarpone*—cream cheese, *à la Italia*—
thickly topped with shavings of bittersweet chocolate:

                      one more
treat we hadn't dreamed existed, that night you led us through
cobbled back streets of Perugia, fearless in shadows deep below
medieval walls built, you told us, on Roman walls built on
what Etruscans left behind:

                 such mysteries, glorious beyond
our simple tourist imaginations that night we dined at your own
favorite restaurant, ordered squash blossom fritters and stuffed
fried olives,

       other surprises picking us up the way that very morning
you'd lifted our spirits with melon, *prosciutto*, four kinds of
bread you'd shopped for before we were even awake:

                   friends of just a few days
feeling we'd known you for years—the way all students and colleagues
in your presence lived vivid and true and full of moment:

all of us trusting that all Dante's circles of Hell mattered no more
than one whose heart you would keep from breaking: the one
wanting to go home early; another whose boyfriend let her down:

none of us dreaming beyond the gift of your life,
that you should take it back
without notice.

Beyond comprehension, these divers
picking you up, out of the river.

Your own layers of grief beneath all of that love,
impossible. None of us dreaming it there.

After a Class in Seaweed

These names like exotic diseases—*Alaria, Porphyra,
Fucus*—or terms transmitted from darkrooms (try
Iridia, try *Laminaria*). Still, it's hard to
imagine our world's future food supply
blessed with names like bullwhip kelp, though
that's what it looks like, and history shows

maiden's hair is poisonous, leaving us
(if we stick with the representational) sea
palm and lettuce—high in iron, potassium,
iodine, protein, you name it—and once you see
how good they can taste, who knows, you might
impress your friends with your daring, you might

start a new trend. Believe me, these new scientist
cooks know what they're up to. Last week I stir-fried
some kind of algae with onions, green peppers, garlic
and soy sauce. Forgot it wasn't spinach. Tried
Porphyra chips with salsa, disguising an aftertaste
clinging like limpets, like shriveled up slug trails

that don't wash off. Anything's possible. Like
tonight, the casserole I took to the potluck
full of sea palms everyone took to be diced
black olives (smothered with hamburger, tucked
into a sauce of tomato and cheddar). Like finding
good intentions not only tricking the tongue, but blinding.

In the Tradition of Good Intentions

When in doubt—don't, but truly, Kate,
how could I doubt you'd like the *springerle* forms I stumbled

onto in Freiburg's open-air market: hand-carved rolling pin, almost
the same designs as my own at home, and three, hand-carved

rectangular molds: woodcutter, angel, cherub. Yes,
I knew they were also a gift for the kitchen, what

you'd make would be not only your own.
But all these years of sending you cookies

each December, our private tradition, knowing you
never, ever, could bake your own. Where in Cherry Valley

could you have found the molds?

And now you say you've always looked forward
to them. Now, I won't be sending them.

Ever since then it's been on my mind.
And this story you've heard me tell:

how, when you were three weeks old (Thanksgiving) I wanted to
share all my 3-D Viewmaster's wonders. I held the clunky box

so carefully over your eyes. I never dreamed
it could slip and bump your brows. How you cried, and Mother

came running. Sister, believe me, I never wanted to hurt you.
I wasn't thinking through your eyes at all.

Doors

1.
A modern door could get tired of bluffing.
Put your ear to its chest. Rap lightly.
Pockets of air tremble from skin to skin.

2.
Doors in this old house are solid: walnut, fir, oak,
who knows? Fifty years of white enamel, each layer
additional armor for weathering scrutinous eyes.

3.
A door could get tired of having two faces.
A door could get tired of having no face of its own.

4.
A swinging door is all things to all people.

5.
We have quarreled.
What door plugs neighborhood ears?

6.
Which of our doors will come unhinged?
When will they tire of coming between us?

7.
After the old folks surrendered the house

after MacDonald's sold it to us
after we took off the roof and at 5 a.m. the movers pulled it

three miles across town (Franklin, Eleventh, Willamette, Eighteenth) passing
all official inspections, parked cars, branches, traffic lights swinging

after you bounced full length on the solid glass doors of the early morning donut
    shop
that looked open, and wasn't, our own car idling, our house

gliding away from us, after
placing ladder to porch and with ten-month-old baby finally

we ascended: the front
door wouldn't let us in.

8.
Two a.m. I know a silence
deeper than space: our daughter
sleeping: the other side of this door.

9.
She hangs, one hand on each knob, watching me write this line.
The door swings back and forth, she laughs, she's riding,
she's never done this before.

10.
Doors, try to imagine another house, a girl, the back sides of her hands
pressed hard, hard against the open frame she stands in
counting slow as she can stand it up to ten

stepping outward, rising, her arms
thin spirits all their own, steady as stems,
rising all the way over her head.

The Way It Was

Monday mornings with her mother the girl
    hung out wash in the back yard, under the cherry tree
        next to the playhouse —
        room enough almost to stand in, hold
small table and chairs, a pitcher of Kool-Aid, one

friend who could come over after the wash was hung —
    her mother in house dress, skirt the wind couldn't resist
        whipping, inflating like bubblegum,
        two-masted sail traveling
nowhere farther than sheets anchored with clothespins, one

hand in the cloth–chicken bag from the church bazaar, one
    on the cotton sheet revolving like a door if she'd let it, one
        clamping the next pin in the middle,
        the next on the end, helping
the daughter trying to help to lift the whole sagging line with a prop —

wooden pole notched to fit between sheets, towels, washcloths
    together all in a row. Always the underwear
        out of sight between shirts,
        together. Dresses, together.
Pants, jeans, socks together. That's how they would all come down.

One hand on the ready to slap
    the daughter who might talk back, might question the one
        right way.
        Which has always been known.
And on Tuesdays they ironed.

Fertility Plant

Otherwise known as mother of millions,
who dare question her love of children,
the old woman who lived in the shoe
had it slick. This brood is used

to falling in anywhere — jade plant, coleus —
they even stay small a long time. Of course
not everyone makes it, or this would be called
an invasion: parachute jumpers sprawled

all over your windowsill: crocodile teeth
spilling from leaf edges, bottom jaws, each
tooth for weeks with its roots exposed,
shameless, waiting a pot of its own.

Too busy bearing to bloom, their mother
goes it alone. Single, she's tough, her one
stem ascending high as cathedral scaffolding,
bending sometimes at the knees, holding

on to faith in powers beyond
her control: magic or God: one wand
and hundreds of incarnations just
like mother, hand over fist

rolling like syllables over green edges
serrated like knives: so many blessings
who could refuse to receive each one?
Who would curse each holy ghost of a tongue?

And the Greatest of These

Can you blame me?
      my mother at eighty-five asks, telling
            why she hung up on the friend who said she wanted to be

up front, who won't take rides any more with my mother,
      who dared to say she doesn't feel safe —
            What is the loving child to do?

God will see you, even if I
      don't, is what she taught, the tongue
            I'd stuck out behind her back like Little Lulu at Tubby but

wouldn't you know it, the first time ever, she caught me,
      and caught me at lying, which leads to stealing and stealing,
            certain as everything Grandfather taught her, to murder.

And later, I must have been ten, my eyes
      red from once again trying to sponge up her fury, my eyes
            I hid in the restroom at school, so no one (*Good girls don't tell*

what happens at home) would see, not even the teacher I longed to
      confide in, and didn't, even when later she asked me.
            So certain I was, doing the very right thing.

On the Nature of Bach's B Minor Mass

Next to the last performance and Nancy,
crying, can't help it: how can anything
ever be this big again. Trish too,
who until this morning has never
forgotten to fix breakfast, her husband
saying this singing must fill her right up.

Stranger than fiction, my mother would say.
Last week a soprano whose name I still don't know
looked right through me at Sears
Auto Parts store and tonight you'd think we were old
friends, kept from each other by seating
arrangements no one thought about changing any

more than notes in a score: faces closed
tight as zero, such concentration, no one
knew anyone's name, where in the world
we'd later show up: Observer Graphics, rummage
sales, the meter maid wagon, outside of your own
kid's school a father whose kid goes there too.

Last night Nathan surprised me, went on about Noah,
newborn, named because in one look he saw a son
strong enough to live up to a name and Noah is
a name to live up to: opening
strangers up to each other—on sidewalks,
in stores—stopping because of a baby who knows

nothing except love, *love*, a word so total
to question it is absurd. Turning our heads,
this music tonight against all we ever have learned
of decorum (*Sanctus! Gloria!*), Bach's postulation
of such absolute form tonight again releasing us,
binding us, this magnificent counterpoint of control.

Armistice

The strongest of all warriors are these two—Time and Patience.
— Leo Tolstoy, *War and Peace*

All their lives the girl studied the mother.
This was her favorite subject, the one she
was best in, there was nothing

about their history of battle the girl
did not remember: which words could turn into
land mines, how to keep her distance and still

appear loving, appear sweet, how much
of independent thought to sacrifice for
a truce that never would last, her heart

from an early age taking a break each time it was
called upon to perform, no allies in place
to protect it, no trench. After your death

I say it: I was that girl. You were that mother.
Now, the small unexpected bells of forgiveness
ringing, ringing, calling me

to attention: what made you
someone to love. All along. I loved you.
And was too busy practicing defense to see.

Mother's Day, Ellensburg, Washington

Next to me at the counter, a woman, a stranger
compliments our waiter on his tie:

imperial crests perched
like red and black chickens
too big for the roost: out of place
among hash browns and toast as I was last night

reading mother and daughter poems to college students
in this high desert oasis where children are not
where it's at and mothers are who you have to
be seen with at breakfast during this annual visit.

So why my surprise when the waiter suddenly beams,
becomes voluble; tells, although I can't hear, what is surely

his favorite tie story before moving on to refill my tea
and converse as though I were not old enough to be his own
mother: I, who at eighteen thought twenty-one
unapproachable; twenty-one, thought the faculty

wife with toddlers already was over the hill; who just
this morning has been looked through by just such another
young woman, her eyes on a future vague as glamour surely
lying beyond this tedium of courtesy, beyond this plain, blatant day.

And why am I suddenly grateful, as I found myself just
last week in the store when a clerk I'd never met, exclaimed

What a beautiful jacket! and I saw she was talking to me.
And why, less than an hour ago, asking directions of the older-
than-middle-aged filling station attendant, didn't I follow
my impulse to ask where she got that peach-colored orchid on

her lapel, so she could maybe have told me one of her children
gave it to her; so she could have had someone to tell? Such
simple things, really: these moments of pleasure I keep on learning
are *yes*, each day in our power to give each other, to help

keep this inescapable human circle in repair, keeping
each of us, as the lucky among us once were kept in the eyes
of our own mothers, visible. Whole.

II.

The signals we give — yes, or no, or maybe —
should be clear: the darkness around us is deep.

—William Stafford
from "A Ritual to Read to Each Other"

Visiting Central School

Driving the freeway north from Eugene
each morning the scenery shifts:

lambs sprout through fields that
yesterday swayed only with sheep,

white faces of calves shine like stars too new
to be named, the green of their sky

startling. Deep. Or fog
hides everything,

hugs the earth so tight I think
it will never let go.

Golden as forsythia branches,
sunlight always

somewhere breaks through.
Magic happens

every day of our lives.
We can grow up, and still see it.

Synchronicity

Back in that rustic laundry cabin doubling as Wurlitzer library
Yes, I could have carried back to my rooms that book by Jung
Yes, I saw it lying there unshelved, next to our communal
Washer and dryer, left by another artist I'd still to meet
Like me in retreat from the everyday world of phones and programs

Because I have big things to write
Because I've brought my notes for a series on *Death*
And the Maiden I used to be, notes on the Holocaust, Catholic
Saints, because I'd already checked out a book of poems
By someone who almost

Became a friend when we were students
Thirty years back but he left to teach in a state
Impossibly far away, our paths crossing (I'm told) on lips
Of friends and here, now, on a shelf in this remote artist's retreat
Where it seems he also (years ago) came to write, and if that

Isn't synchronicity, what is?

And though I briefly remark to myself on this
And though a magpie calls to me from the tree outside
A flicker swoops greetings, and though a house finch trills
In the wind remarking my absence, my mind
Is happily already elsewhere. I almost

Don't take a moment to talk to the stranger who's just
Now parking outside, who's taken this moment between Denver and Santa
Fe to visit someone no longer here, and tells me he almost came
The day before (before I arrived) and just now almost didn't stop
Having lingered too long at a rock shop, as I

Myself almost lingered over the Jung but said to myself
No, be resolute: three thousand miles you've traveled to be here

Three years of planning. Not knowing I'd taken just the right amount of
Time for the laundry, finishing just five minutes ago and no
Sooner, or yes, I would be already back in my cabin

Never dreaming how close I'd have come to crossing paths with a stranger
Whose name is, yes, the name on the book in my hand
Whose wonder, like mine, could go on like planets in separate orbits
Forever. Unfolding, unfolding, as in *The Living Desert*
Where flowers open right under our eyes.

Love in Venice

1.
Common knowledge, now, that in the Sámi language
in Norway, in Sweden, Finland, Russia, more than a hundred
words exist for different kinds of snow.

Our Sámi friend Harald says there might be even more words for
different ways to jump.

And in our language, yours and mine: "to come,"
what words? And who
could possibly count?

2.
And did you, like me, question the teacher insisting
no two snowflakes are ever alike?

No two chromosomes, no two grains of sand. Stars
in galaxies still to be fathomed. Twenty-

seven, nearly twenty-eight years of being with you,
the visions blazing within our coming each time

unpredictable. New. Who ever said
it could still be like this?

3.
Titian's angel in *The Annunciation* that vortex of gold orange pink red in which those
same-colored wings emerge from muscular clouds firm biceps of Michelangelo's
David the nest of his armpit firm smooth white cumulus chest muscles gleaming
votive red the censors the candles red constellations of candles splitting the dark of
St. Mark's basilica golden domes of the cupolas and all around us all of this color
color color color

4.

Have you thought about this: nothing stops
the common sparrow from constant chirping, morning till night.

Not the thrashing of rain, of daytime thunder.
Not the summer oven of sun, or cats on prowl. This afternoon,

Before we made love, talking softly together,
as usual, I heard them.

There they are again.

Naked

Okay, let them think we never were young and daring
never writing of sheets streaked with come

see how I've held my tongue, never telling how years ago we took
everything off and swam behind bushes in a public

picnic ground of a national park. Or once again how
beyond the gaze of neighbors, cut off from news in a trailer

bound by three feet of country snow, I first made you
snow angels, hollows scooped from the crests of drifts my arms

scraped like sky, like spellbound waves our dog (our
sunflower, sand-colored swimmer, his fur a cluster of berries

white in a bush of fire) plowed trails through, spelling
what scent he knew, nosing frozen foam to find a snowball

white on white as one as your skin and mine the night we dared
frost and the moon, two shivering question marks, periods buried,

luminous (your thighs your chest your face and) the face of the snow
we tossed at each other like clouds, like waves exploding, bearing us

into our own motion again, to sleeping bag blankets,
warm sheets, to our mouths.

Fan Letter from the Fourth Grade

You're big, he says.
He says he didn't know
that first day of class my poems
were published, the fact
I'd written a book. He says,
Would you like some candy?
and his hand works out of his jeans
pocket a lavender heart, its edges
worn down like chalk by who
knows how many washings: *Hot Stuff,*
Cool Cat, Ask Me, May I, whatever
words that were anyway only for fun, erased.

Reserve

1.
I loved it: we'd never met and the famous
poet years ago answered my first fan letter,
closing with *Love,*

2.
Despite our mutual dislocation, despite
many months of acquaintance and dinners
and the fact that my former colleague and I part
now, each time with a hug

Still she signs her letters *Warmly,* or
With affection. As ever. Yours. Once
just last week, I took the big step
signed an e-mail message, *Love,*

Fond regards, she replied.
As ever.

3.
And can it be true we once confessed
to each other (this very same colleague, or friend
as really, she is, I think) each of us had been suffering

European aloofness: the way strangers would never
smile on the street, the way clerks in stores didn't ask
how you were, although of course we knew it was silly to care,

Why should it matter, this small talk, but still (wouldn't you know)
we each had invented a private game of purposely smiling first,
seeing who, if anyone, dared smile back. And sometimes, ha ha, it worked.

And can it be true this same friend, over wine, once said
That waiter is surly, let's try to make him smile. Did she know

he spoke English? That he was in hearing? Did she see his face?

4.
Will I show my friend this poem?

Likeness

Of this only snapshot of you forever
walking away
(sea foam shreds
of a letter around you,
filigree concrete bridge in front of you)
I could say *fitting*: this landscape the same
one your showed me in one of your own
photos, years back.

And then I showed it to you —
added a crab lunch, beach
stones to crack it with,
wine and a gust of rain that sent you
back to the car for coats.
Later we took ourselves to where nothing
again would happen and like
before we knew why.

"Why must I always be saying
good-bye to you?" you wrote,
"I love you," you wrote and even
these words you took back again like a kite
reeled in, gone too far.
Like before. That pattern of self-
denial together the most
tangible thing we had.

Repartee

Our eyes perceive the world in the language of light.
—*National Geographic* TV special

Choosing what not to say when each word is a step in the dark,
sometimes takes too long and then there is trouble. No matter

that you, who always try to look out for their toes, try
also not to step on your own, a position

no longer in fashion, today the word is *speed*, it's leaping
into revolving responses like doors

no one need exit from, no one need hear anyone else. Oh,
how we admire the quick ones their verbal *jujitsu*, seeing it all in the flash

of a strobe light, flipping us over their shoulders like salt, for good luck.
Distortions? No matter. To be ready with answers even before

hearing the questions! Surely it's only chance that writing these lines,
not knowing where they were going, I took a break, turned on the TV,

saw a leap of proof to give me heart. And take it away.
And give it back again.

Studies with computers show what discus throwers take
on faith: force

is lost on the ground by not rigidly planting the feet.
The tortoise-hare principle, all

over again. Plato's
cave. Like trees in the forest,

our sturdiest words falling
on deaf ears.

Split Couplets for John

Wind from the north and this morning the mountaintops vanished
In show, a forecasted

Coming: this month, this day of saying good-bye.
But not that the sky

Would be so clear for such a somber business.
Instead of stillness

Birds on the hillside are trilling their hearts
Away. It's hard

To reconcile cadence and content. Varenna brilliant across
The lake. The loss

Of your promise among us.

Some Words to Toss Your Direction

Call if the going gets rough, and always
the promise, *I will.* This

ritual has gone on for years. And still,
in these everyday waters that keep on rising over our heads,

one or the other keeps floundering, one or the other keeps
watch: twice

down, never a third or the cry
for rescue, this distance perhaps

the way of all balance, no need
for us both to go down. And still

the longing: one word of knowing
someone knows, tossed

out without a line to pull us back in,
without a thought to consequence.

One bright rescue helping us want to go on.

Jade Plant in Split Couplets

Slower to speak than a temple of stone, this green
shrine keeping

faith with our good intentions, despite neglect;
a self-respect,

a balance we know we can count on. Firm stance,
constant as

four seasons, planets in orbit, the moon,
this sage is in tune

with something no eye can detect: ceaseless
this green stasis:

leaf opposite leaf, soul bared to soul.
That tugging, that musical

Pull! The deepest tide, our blood, its hum.
Forever, this Om.

All We Can Use

— for Enid

Here is one more poem you're part of: meanings
your life has for someone else holding
the pen, circling

back from where you intended the day
you showed me his poem with your
name in it, proof

of your loss, what you still
would hold on to, your
side of the story

absent as even my own name was in someone
else's poems: words about me,
touching me where his hands

refused, his actual silence I took
for necessary salt, curing all
expectations like years

of unspoken promises neither of us could
break, although we walked in that
same place

that summer dress was mine.
Once I tried to respond: *I confess*
to a thousand confessions

of as many somewhat friends
to a washing of selves like silver
of words like solvent on the skin

hedging my bets behind sounds abstract
as a recipe, good at least to read

in case nothing

was real, words I share to show
what can be used again, without
exploitation. Regret

is a luxury, ripe as bananas,
good only for bread,
for this new

poem for you, made from
what can be saved
too long.

Tree of Joy at the Super

Mal (*better watch out*) the mystery

Mal (*better not pout*) who's asked for
"A Beautiful Doll" — not Barbie, not Felicity, not American Girl

Mal's red felt heart on the tree in the same
Delicate script as all the other requests, and your own
Heart goes out: that awkward print beneath, "NOT PAPER"

Mal never suspecting you,
The finder, would wonder how old
Is this child? What doll is suitable? You or
Someone might check with Foster Care Services

Naughty Mal whose name never was
On the list Foster Care brought to Food
Value, each name with its age and its Christmas
Wish transcribed
Each heart

Dangling. Mal? the store manager puzzles, Mal?
(*I'm asking you twice*) Our maintenance man?
Mal's heart, eighty years old
Is caught.

Return it, the manager says, Exchange it.
And all the dangling questions: who
The needful? who the child?

Mal's heart in your hand.
What's naughty?

What's nice?

To a German Painter Who Asked
about Poetry's Open Forms

You show me your rhythms I'll show you
mine, the way certain intervals
beyond the measure
of time unfurl
and fluctuate: no
tango no march but like your own
clear plastic "Time Stations" intersecting

tomorrow on paths no signpost has access to

no computer command to interface
daffodils trumpets angels and swordfish but here
they are anyway: psalms of images each with its own refrain
the echo of rune on rune: layer of paint on paint: shapes of stellae, steeples
tombstones reaching into the past and the past repeating: mass
graves and our own and fractals of history shifting:
patterns not in the motion itself but in
the measure between:

flotsam and jetsam love's leftovers: spaces in which the spirit sings

stage lights spot lights overlapping the way tomorrow is shining through
yesterday: white yellow orange gold *Amsel* rooster robin *Kiebitz*
and somewhere a cow you hear them all
in the same
moment and we know what
comes next: this measure we follow a helix a spiral
crescendo cresting nothing to do with clocks with yardsticks with limits with stop.

This Is His Story:

Who years ago started collecting
stories of others

Who now surrounds himself with their stories like stones

Who finds them all beautiful: polished and smooth,
the petrified, fossilized, rough puffs of lava

Whose travels across the vast landscapes of feeling
wear holes in his pockets, his wife can't keep up with them
friends can't get through to him

Who answers questions by holding up yet someone else:
friend

Whose whole
life has become all of
this holding together

Who started by knowing the spirit
is truly a slippery place.

Reader, put this in your pocket: this tale
of a friend who once was, and is gone.

Silence

After a painting by Odilon Redon, 1911

Caught at last in this brown caution,
this wake of sound beyond the known
alphabet, where is our refuge?

Frame of forgetting.
Frame of remembering.
Floor of a faith forever gone.

Steps we've taken, those footprints
are in us forever. Listen.
All those words we never will say, echoing.

III.

We reach forth and strain every nerve, but we seize
only a bit of the curtain that hides the infinite from us.

—Maria Mitchell, astronomer

O to be delivered from the rational into the realm of pure song.

—Theodore Roethke
from "What Can I Tell My Bones?"

Requiem for a Soprano

Somewhere off the coast of Greenland, high in the North
Sea, there's a giant white swirl in the water
Of what can only be thousands

No, millions of icebergs that from this airplane
Window look no larger than pinpricks, starry white
Speckles on blue immense as the night

Sky without a moon, as though God has taken
A giant finger over the water's surface, whirled it white,
A whole new galaxy, too

Vast to be named. Song
Could get lost in a space like this.

Or fill it.

Your voice, no longer among us.
The gift that was your life
Echoing.

With Ninety-Eight Friends

Counting, counting, every ninth wave is bigger they say, and here on the western
edge of this continent once again off and on all day I've tried to see if it's true.

Across the whole earth the terrible countdown continues.
Ten hours till midnight, and all the world betting on who will be first

to back down: two countries for whom the cost of face saved has already
been counted, the word "casualty" just today by the media re-

defined: not to be confused with how many really will die.
Across the whole earth the terrible countdown continues.

How many troops are in place. Missiles. Body bags. How the president's
chaplain has prayed for peace, the president already at peace with himself.

How we count on the checkout clerk at Safeway to tell us to have a nice day
and the words will hang between us, bait caught by a fish no one wants.

And when the war comes and surely before we have news of it
out of our hearing the shrieks of missiles, children, sirens: knowing

death is coming but not on whom it will fall,
I will be back in town, rehearsing with ninety-eight friends the notes of Brahms'

Requiem—Was soll ich mich trösten?—having watered the house plants,
fed the cat who will vomit again and the question will be when,

not if, we will put him to sleep—having phoned a friend on whom death
may also be falling, who has been waiting for x-ray reports, years of coming

uncertainty lived in one day. *Was soll ich mich trösten?*
These tangible, unavoidable griefs one wave in the ocean ahead.

Numbers

Poem ending with words by William Stafford

Iris says there's safety in numbers, when

someone else arrives to share the house she won't
need to lock the door

When did Iris last read the news?

&

And did you, like me (age nine? age ten?), try

dividing the total number of babies
born in one whole year (how many was it?) by

all the days in the year, by twenty-four hours,
by sixty minutes, sixty seconds, oh!

So many new babies in one single second!

(Any thought of how many new dead?)

&

Now, what do we do with these numbers?

The five largest airline disasters, in order
Uncovered, the biggest mass graves to date
Whoever is leading in thousands killed
(Iraq, ourselves, Afghanistan, Palestine, Israel)

How many less were lost in the towers than first
reported.

Numbers *being* the news.

&

Earthquake, Haiti: two hundred
thousand dead, government sources say, or maybe
two-fifty

Two million homeless, three million
needing emergency aid

More than the great
Indian Ocean tsunami, how high

Reader, must the number be for us
to say it's time

To contribute?

Three miles away, I saw them
burning, saw one
go down
went
for my phone
came back
the other
was gone

Well, I
was three *blocks*
away, saw people running

I was *across the street*
saw people
jumping

Well, I had an afternoon meeting planned
right there

Before the broadcast of body bags returning
was banned

Five weeks before "Shock
and Awe," at least

Six, the BBC said, and maybe ten million people protested in sixty
countries around the world on one
single weekend.

According to Guiness, the protest in Rome:
three million alone: the largest
anti-war rally in history.

Sixty-five thousand Iraqi civilians killed
since 2003, or one hundred seven
thousand (different sources, take
your pick). Our war

is on Terror, not
that country. Repeat, we are not
at war with that country.

Is this what the people of that country believe?

And now, the need for an increase in troops,
the only question: ten thousand? twenty?
thirty?

And now, the suicide increase in troops
returning, the largest
percentage ever.

And here, the homeless vet on the corner.

Here, the Cottage Grove family's telegram triggering
earthquakes, aftershocks

rumbling
all the rest of their lives.

꩜

*Imagine life is a great big seesaw and each of us
a grain of sand.*

*Your job: to put your grain of sand
where it belongs.*

*You never know which grain will be the one that tips it
in the right direction.* (Pete Seeger, in concert.)

꩜

Here's how to count the people who are ready to do right:
"One." "One." "One."

One of Those Things

If God made everything, who made God? I ask them, and *How on earth*
do storks get babies into the hospital? Anyone else, I ask, *ever have questions*
like this? The ones grownups

don't know how to answer? And with them it's easy, this playing with wonder,
keeping alive what knowledge would have us deny.
Together we rescue the Right

Brain: students the age of my own daughter, the son I never had, writing,
Why don't fish drown? Where does the black of the night sky begin? Myself
still unable to grasp how the sky just keeps on going, or how

the reliable sea could just last week become
other: oil spreading from just one tanker farther than any human
vision: birds, fish, otters washing ashore in numbers like stars

all of us long ago stopped
trying to count.

Today not asking where but when it will end: that infinite sea
with all its unknowns, once within the grasp of what we still could imagine,
grounding us.

One of those things we knew was forever, for sure.

Lesson Plans, Vernal, Utah

1.
Driving to class this morning, recalling Miss Thomas
(who asked me to write my own first poem), who, now that I think of it,
must have been younger than I am right now— oh, the strangeness, children
looking at me, thinking I have grown up!

2.
How many of us have looked at photos of pioneer settlers:
their faces so frozen, so bug-eyed (how hard they challenge
the camera: who'll be first

to blink?): all my life
they could have been thirty or fifty, how would I know, and now
they're younger than my own friends.

All those years thinking everyone older
knew better: that deep
habit of letting them know what's right.

Still stranger: years ago finding
that first policeman younger than me.

3.
Whoever has been to the quarry at Dinosaur National Monument
twenty-some miles northeast of this town, learns
how much older is this earth than anything
we can imagine.

Older than teachers, or grandparents.
Older than whoever taught those
grandparents' grandparents.

Older than stories. People before
Butch Cassidy. Cassidy's hideout: barbed wire

the Wild Bunch in Devil's Hole strung between trees,
now swallowed by bark.

Older than trees. Even bones
scientists still
chip out of the mountain,

those dinosaur tibiae, fibulae, vertebrae, skulls, are still
not as old as the ribs of the earth
tilted skyward,

those petrified, fossilized, many-colored skeletons
Grave-Robber Green River slashed
up and out of Split
Mountain. All

that change.
So much that's been here all along.

4.
Those lines above, did you notice the metaphors?
I didn't say *old as the hills*. You're right, that's *clichè*, and besides,
it's hills I'm talking about:

that Drive Through the Ages, cars
in the canyon spiraling upward past signs:

Carmel Formation (dinosaurs roamed here);
Mancos Formation (home of fossilized squid);

Chinle, Madison, Curtis, Lodore (in one of these,
crocodile teeth). In the Morgan Formation,
shellfish preserved in stone.

5.
One of my new friends, a woman I met in her forties, once
showed me a picture of high school beauty queens.
Can you find me? she asked.
I was lucky. I could.

At my twenty-fifth high school reunion
how I wanted to bless the classmate who planned
we all should wear name tags: kind flashlights to steer us
until our eyes had grown used to the dark
until the souls of the people we knew
shone through.

6.
All those years of assuming "grown up" meant
having to be someone else.

I remember a tale of a girl each morning
drinking a fresh cup of dew.

Each day she grew smaller.
You're tempted to try it?

So was I.
Three years old, I cried

the night before my next birthday.
Why? my father wanted to know.

Tomorrow I'd be too old
ever again to bounce on his knee.

7.
How much we change.

And how little. Children,
listen, for years
I've been waiting to write this poem.

Where was it? These details—the photographs,
high school reunion, my father—remember? All
this time they have been right here, waiting

the way deer stand by the side of the road
then bolt,

the way raindrops build to a flash flood slicing
straight to the core.

And your own
memories: what your own children and their
children's children someday will hear:

what you bring to each classroom
together,

what you bring out
in each other, the selves

you are who will not
disappear, remembering
maybe this day when

together we inhabited moments of grace,
imagination tilting our earth
just a little,

dreams roaming our papers, our pencils
uncovering thoughts we didn't know were still
with us: this day

another layer between
what comes after
and what has already come before.

This fragile soil.

Give Us This Day

Just as everyone knows the end might come without warning
Any morning, the usual intersection and someone running the light,
Or maybe a gun in the cafeteria. Suitcase exploding. Fuselage
Simply missing one simple bolt. And we know not
To dwell on these thoughts, to survive.

Just as when my older friend was dying, and knew it, saying
I've learned what I wish I'd known all my life, and I wanted to
Know her secret and didn't ask, so sure of having one last chance.
This much I've learned: *Savor it. This daily bread.*
What if this were our last day alive?

So, too, you with your own secret ticking, lab tests predicting
Tomorrow the beats all of us count on could stop.
With proper exercise, diet, maybe
Not for a year. Or two.
Or more.

Each moment, remember. Each moment, forget.
Systole. Diastole.
Push. Pull.
Dear one,
Whose heart knows and won't tell.

Losing in the Mail My Years-Old Copy
of Your Specially Autographed Book

As when my father died and I wasn't
as I had intended, holding his hand,
was taking care, instead, of my mother at home:
cooking supper, doing the dishes, before returning to
his hospital bed, that one hour, only, all day
and that was the hour, of course, he died,
alone, although the nurses said they had been in the room
right then, turning him over, how easy
to catch that small, well-meaning,
deception
                — last summer in Frankfurt I didn't
want to think about packing the box again.
I wanted to trust the post office clerk who said
the box would be perfectly safe, tied up only in
string, let him slit the tape, it would be so
much cheaper. True. And the office was closing,
I was leaving tomorrow morning, my suitcase already
too full. And nothing that precious could ever
truly be lost if I willed it not so.

Beyond Argument

Of course, there's always this other side: whole
cultures in which the only right way to leave this earth
is to burn, quickly: the Big Bang backwards, each
cell simultaneously sizzling, exploding; the body
sputtering into itself like a galaxy given the names
Practical, Cheaper; that willful black hole of the body taken
beyond argument, out of its own human element, finally
under some human control.

So when my mother asks me to remember her wishes,
when she tells me arrangements are made, what
can I say? Three days, she tells me, the soul
stays in the body; we mustn't burn her too soon.

And when four years back we handed my father over
to fire, I was at home with my mother among all the flowers and
casseroles, neighbors and friends, eating peanuts, not
asking the time of its happening, or where.

This is survival.
These things, I have no choice but accept.

Yet how much better it seems to let the body go on being
body, free to perform in its own good time that last
deliberate act, which belongs to it, which is its right,
to slowly go back into the earth,

keeping pace with the long process of mourning,
reversing the days before speech, before thought, instinctive
the blind groping of cells down to that wild, predictable
dance of atoms circling fires that will burn and keep on
burning until anyone left in this world who remembers, is gone.

Though this, too, like the farthest edge of the sky, is beyond
comprehension: these flickering
words I speak as though they will always be heard.

Ashes on the Tongue

1.
Two years, my silence,
and what can I say to explain it,
your name still hasn't appeared.

Cricket words pecking the dark.
White noise of cicadas all day long.

Brain dead, they told me, and still
that whole long day you kept on breathing
I sang to you, talked to you.

Words couldn't keep you.
What now can I say that will count?

2.
Such comfort we took in convention.
The way you shined all our shoes each Sunday,
wore nothing but laundry-starched shirts.
The way we knelt each night to say prayers,
hands folded around our words,
words folded around my heart.

And these things are part of me.
How at the office your overtime paid for not
joining the small talk. Your horror
at finding the business course guide to success:
love of money comes first;
choose only those friends who can help you.

3.
So much to choose from, telling a life. What
comes first? What one thing says it all?

Too sick for the service, I said no eulogy.
Friends, family wondered:

she whose business
is words.

Your ashes I've taken on faith
buried somewhere I have not yet been.

4.
Some days, this certainty: only a few words,
by saying them, cancel what's left.
And if all of them matter the same?

Nine reels of tape we made that last winter,
your voice fixing stories to places and friends
none of the rest of us knew.

Oh, vigilant memory!
All these candles my own words would light!

One for the boy for whom chariots seared the sky.
One for the cavalry officer cleaning the stalls.
One for the swimmer surprised by the walrus.
One for the immigrant on the assembly line,
daily the new English words in the hand,
the diligent foot right on beat.

One whole cathedral ablaze with your life!

Last week I heard a new poet, a stranger.
One hour, the places she spoke came alive.
People we will not remember, that hour only
were with us; yet this

remains: the way joy
circled her grief and her voice
rang

pure and true.
This moment, it called to me

Worshiper,
this is where we are now.

5.
Some days things come together, come clear,
The way observances matter: communions.

Insistent, they pull me awake.
Sunlight. Birds at the feeder.

Look what things I've known and forgotten,
What never occurred before!

I think of the film I once saw about Eskimos,
How after a death the ashes are passed
One to another, with honor
Placed on the tongue

If some days I don't speak,
If I don't say your name
    like this

Whenever I speak, may I speak
    like this

With a voice that is partly yours.

A Gathering

... one must let the mind loose to respond as it will, to receive impressions,
to sense rather than know, to gather rather than immediately understand.
—Edward Albee

1. Coma

Most of all I think it was her arm, doubled back at the elbow
and poised, rigid wing, midair, that stopped me, so much

I'd brought to her bedside to tell.
Martina's safe landing, the plane, the full

moon tonight and the fawn with its pebbled
coat fading. A light

touch to ease her dying. To tell her our grief
would not try to hold her back.

As though it could.
As though her turning inward had not

been noticed. What had I been thinking? She, who left
home to get on with this dying.

Who waved goodbye last week
at the door.

Bones, bones, and steady breathing, and hearing
said to be last to go.

2. Change

But how do we jump from the speeding train of our own
good intentions? There I was reading out loud in front of your coma
something I'd folded and stuffed at the last minute into my skirt
pocket, a passage I'd found and typed and planned to send in the mail

in which one of the characters—young, much younger than I—talks about change, not knowing how it happens or what is required but only what it feels like to change. She gives us her great-great-grandmother's words, she gives us *beautiful*. Mary,

what I'd been wanting to say was how, the last time we spoke, I saw that change in your eyes, I'd never seen you so beautiful. That was *my* word, in my own mind, right then. And then I found hers. And by the time I read this passage to you, it didn't reach the two feet between us, already you were no longer there.

3. How I Knew

> *... Dora Rouge said it happens all our lives. She said that we are cocoons who consume our own bodies and at death we fly away transformed and beautiful.*
> —Linda Hogan

Such imminent news and still the blue jay
    Squawked, like any other day, relentlessly.

Grape leaves over my head in the new arbor
    Flickered and swayed, morning sun between them

Flinging itself at the ground and falling forever
    Short, and the book I was reading held me

Just enough so at that moment I was not thinking of
    You, the tiny leaf that landed on my upper sleeve

Was one more small distraction: or was it the dried
    Half of a maple-pip, bright veins the color of rust

And nothing in between: fallen wing I couldn't
    Identify, which bush, which nearby vine

Had leaves like that? And then just as quietly
    As it had come the moth rose and was gone. "Mary,"

I said without thinking, "Mary."
        And waited for the call.

4. Why Not?

If our softest words, spoken into a cellular phone can beam
        out and up to satellites hundreds of miles above us and bounce

Back to ears on the other side of earth in less
        time than it takes to type the word "less"

If we grant to radio waves the power to cross open air between the hill
        with its blinking-red tower, far outside of town, and beam the same

Voices and music right through walls of homes, offices, skyscrapers, cars
        on the freeway moving in different directions, all at the very same time

If invisible waves of impulse, can—like the pitch picked up by ears of dogs—slip
        without our knowing, into spaces inside us, around us, and just

As silently leave,
        why not the spirit?

5. Already Beyond Us

And now our friend Ken, in his dying, sends poems.
New ones, a flurry in these wintry days.

He writes of emptiness and promise.
He writes of writing before sleep.

How to respond, find the words for *good-bye*?

The last time we saw another friend, Joe, just
this past October, he told us he's dying

not because his body's diseased. He's done
what he came on this earth to do. His work is complete.

Yes, but what of our friendship?
Will we ever get enough of Ken's poems?

6. *My Mother as Chickadee*

Well, no, not reincarnation, exactly, nothing
    so lifelong. Rather

The day before she died, my mother, coming home from church, wondered
    was there really anything *There* to look forward to?

Well, I said, if there *is*, come back. Tell us. And two days later,
    there I was on my balcony eating breakfast, under the shade of

Morning glories strung to the roof when a flock of six or eight chickadees
    skimmed the air right over my head, were soon out of sight. But one

Turned back, perched on the overhead twine and looked right down, in my
    direction, cocked its little black-capped head

Back and forth, back
    and forth

And flew on.
    (Why not?)

7. *Beyond Us*

And what of our good friend Joe? On that final visit I told him
about my mother. The bird. And how for almost a year my mother came

Not as a bird (never again) to visit every night, just
after I'd settled, as usual, into bed with a book, just after

Ralph was asleep: the lightest pounce
at the foot of the bed

The weight of a cat,
but there wasn't a cat, there wasn't any

72

Thing to see at all. Who will believe this?
How can a poem get by with such nonsense? Such

Hocus-pocus? Still, the day Joe left us, as law allowed,
with Susan and three grown children

Around him—a Steller's jay, royal blue with its pointed crown shiny
black as obsidian—kind of jay that never in all the twenty-five years

We've lived in this house has come so far from woods to town—skipped
from branch to branch just outside of our window, looking

In. And that very same night
on the foot of our bed, a pounce.

8. A Gathering

Days and days burdened
with what I've often impressed on students: write

as though it's for someone with only a short time to live, make it worthy
(good theory)

and then last night, my head on the pillow, re-reading
Ken's poem, his custom of putting pen to paper last thing before sleep,

this flurry: the pounce, the birds, the leaf, my mother, what I never
before would have dared tell the world.

Benediction

As it was in the beginning, is now and ever shall be.

Because I'd once been told what women always had done—though never
how, or why—after you died, the last tube taken out and gone,
and they offered to leave us alone, I asked if I could wash you.

The soapy water was warm, as you were, still, and soft. The basin was round.
The towels and washcloths thick and white. And there was no strangeness in it,
really. And I didn't cry, and that, too, was part of the wonder.

I began with one smooth, pliant arm. As once you daily must have done with me,
as once you must have done at your own mother's death, I carefully dipped one
    cloth,
and carefully wrung it, and carefully bathed the whole freckled length of your arm,

your docile hand, each finger light in its yielding.
And though you had no choice in acquiescing to my love, I did not
revel in my power, but slowly lifted, washed and patted dry each limb, in turn,

your crooked toes and in between the toes; your shoulders, breasts,
the secret folds between your legs, thin pubic hairs, and with a different cloth,
which would have been your way, your face.

I took my time. I lingered in this unexpected absence of condition or demand.
And when at last with nothing more to do, I sat beside your bed and took
the hand I'd long since lost the need to hold, and laid my grown-up hand inside:

Oh, familiar shape my fingers knew by heart and had forgotten
that they'd ever known. How long this total rightness had been gone.
And, as leisurely as once I must have done, when simple being was enough

to please you, I let my eyes, without distraction, wander every
tiny detail of your face, its astonishing calm. I saw again your chin,
unguarded; saw your knuckles worn, arthritic; sang a tune that came

74

from who knows where: *This is the hand that fed me,*
Hand that held me, Hand that punished me, Hand that led me.
For hours, sunlight was the only thing that moved. And soon

would be gone. And your hand in mine, still warm!
I stood to kiss your forehead. It was cold. But I had been
in the presence of holiness. World without end. And was done.

Sanctuary

As flocks of birds from the depths of the field rise
        in unison,   arc and wheel and dip
                with no one bird in the lead
        and settle again into land

As fish in their silent schools flash
        silver together:
                pivot and pivot again on the same
        invisible axis

When the music begins and we, in our separate
        sections, stop
                that inner, ever-
        present mental chatter and join

Together in song, again I forget
        that in the last election
                the second
        soprano next to me almost certainly voted wrong

That in tomorrow's headlines the next
        suicide bomber will take away more
                lives than any one
        heart can mourn. That in the next

Town a friend lies dying, that global
        warming tomorrow will give us
                yet one more
        extinction. Here,

Flood waters rising will threaten
        no one.
                Tenderness rises
        and is not scorned or shunned.

Anger on the horizon crashes and rolls,
    breaks without mercy
        over our heads and no
    harm is done.

What is sacred space if not this shelter of song?
    What is prayer if not these measures
        in which the heart
    can pour itself out, out, out, and the notes

Will catch it, help bear it along? Moments in which
    each wounded and fragmented self
        abides again in the wonder of wholeness.
    Here. In this place. This home.

Notes

"Valse Triste" (Sad Waltz) is the title given to several well-known musical compositions, including one for solo piano by Frédéric Chopin (Waltz No. 3 in A Minor, Opus 34, No. 2); an orchestral piece by Jean Sibelius (Opus 44, originally composed for strings); and one for piano and violin by Franz von Vecsey.

"Tiramisù" is in memory of Professor Emmanuel Hazantonis, professor of Italian at the University of Oregon and director of the University of Oregon Summer Program in Perugia, Italy.

"After a Class in Seaweed" owes everything to the great knowledge and pioneer spirit of Evelyn McConnaughey, author of *Sea Vegetables Harvesting Guide and Cookbook*, whose wonderful class I took through the Hatfield Marine Science Center in Newport, Oregon.

"In the Tradition of Good Intentions." *Springerle* are traditional, cream-colored, lemon- and anise-flavored German Christmas cookies, rectangular and/or square, with intricate, raised designs made by pressing a carved, wooden mold onto rolled dough.

Several sections in "Doors" refer to the old house my husband, Ralph Salisbury, and I purchased from a MacDonald's hamburger restaurant, and moved several miles across Eugene, Oregon, to an empty lot, making way for a parking lot. We lived in, landscaped, and worked on it for eight years.

"On the Nature of Bach's B Minor Mass" is dedicated to the Eugene Concert Choir.

"Synchronicity" is for Douglas Lawder.

"Reserve" is dedicated to Alice Schlegel, who has seen this poem.

"Split Couplets for John" was written while sharing a residency with my husband, Ralph Salisbury, at the Rockefeller Conference and Study Center, Bellagio, Italy.

"To a German Painter Who Asked about Poetry's Open Forms" is for Traude Linhardt, of Munich, with whom I worked on a collaborative art-poetry project at the Villa Waldberta, Feldafing, Germany.

"Requiem for a Soprano" is in memory of Sue Williford of the Motet Singers, Eugene, Oregon.

"With Ninety-Eight Friends." *Was soll ich mich trösten:* What comfort have I?

"Numbers." The next-to-last section, which begins "Imagine life is a great big see-saw," is a paraphrase of words spoken in concert by folksinger Pete Seeger. The last lines of "Numbers," words by poet William Stafford, are from his journal entry of 29 June 1993, which appears in the posthumously published book *Every War Has Two Losers: William Stafford on Peace and War*, edited by Kim Robert Stafford.

About the Author

Born of German-Chilean and German-American parents in Aurora, Illinois, Ingrid Wendt began playing the piano at age five and the organ at eleven. A statewide award winner in high school and a church organist, she studied with Frances Sherwood of the Aurora Conservatory of Music, and with Dr. Rudolph Ganz, president of Chicago Music College. Her books of poems have won the Oregon Book Award (for *Singing the Mozart Requiem*), the Yellowglen Award (for *The Angle of Sharpest Ascending*), and the Editions Prize (for *Surgeonfish*). Her first book, *Moving the House*, was chosen for BOA Editions by William Stafford, who also wrote the introduction. A chapbook, *Blow the Candle Out*, was published by Pecan Grove Press. She is the co-editor of two anthologies: *From Here We Speak: An Anthology of Oregon Poetry* and *In Her Own Image: Women Working in the Arts*, and the author of the book-length teaching guide, *Starting with Little Things: A Guide to Writing Poetry in the Classroom*, now in its sixth printing. Other awards include the D. H. Lawrence Award, the Carolyn Kizer Award, and the Distinguished Achievement Award from her alma mater, Cornell College. She has taught in the MFA program of Antioch University Los Angeles and, as a Senior Fulbright Professor and Fulbright Senior Specialist, in Frankfurt am Main and Freiburg, Germany. A popular keynote speaker and a consultant with the National Council of Teachers of English, she has been a visiting poet at colleges and universities and in hundreds of classrooms, grades K–12, and has conducted teacher workshops in the United States and abroad. She currently performs with The Motet Singers, a semi-professional thirteen-voice women's a cappella ensemble in Eugene, Oregon, where she lives with her husband, poet and writer Ralph Salisbury.